Get Ready!

1 Pupil's Book

Felicity Hopkins

Note

Most of the activities in this book are oral. The words printed
in black are there to guide the teacher. Only the words
or letters printed in a colour are for the pupil to read or
recognize.

Oxford University Press

Notes for the teacher

Get Ready! aims to give pupils a feel for English and to establish a sound basis for later learning. Pupil's Book 1 can be used alone or in conjunction with the Activity Book, Handwriting Book and Numbers Book. A cassette has recordings of all the dialogues and songs in the Pupil's Book. Where an item has been recorded a cassette symbol (▱) appears in the Pupil's Book.

Oral work

Most of the work based on Pupil's Book 1 is oral. Only the words or letters printed in a colour are for the pupil to read. The words in black are there to guide the teacher.

The pictures are to help the pupil, and the teacher should encourage the pupils to point to the pictures when reciting rhymes or singing songs. The expressions shown in the Language Summary do not all appear in the text of the Pupil's Book, but they should be used orally by the teacher. The Picture Practice pages are designed to practise vocabulary and these expressions. The Teacher's Book provides detailed notes on when to introduce them.

Reading

There is no 'real' reading in *Get Ready! 1* but pupils will learn to recognize the letters of the alphabet and know the sound each one makes. They will also learn some whole words and acquire left-right orientation. These first reading skills are developed in both the Pupil's Book and the Activity Book.

The alphabet

It is suggested that the sounds of the letters should be taught first of all, using the formula 'a' for apple, 'b' for boy, etc. The names of the letters can be taught later, through exercises in the Activity Book.

The approach

The teacher should use choral and individual repetition and question and answer routines. Whenever possible, pupils should take on the role of the teacher and ask the questions. Games, such as the one in Step 14, are particularly suitable for this.

The songs are a very important element of *Get Ready!* and teachers should regularly use songs from earlier in the course. While singing, pupils should point to the pictures or perform the suggested actions. These reinforce meaning as well as make learning more enjoyable. Do not expect pupils to understand *every* word in the songs.

Accuracy

Do not be too concerned about accuracy. *Get Ready!* progresses slowly and pupils will gradually become aware of small differences and more able to imitate the teacher's model. Never try to explain language rules to very young learners.

Mother tongue

Most of the lesson should be in English but do use the pupils' own language when it would be helpful. You might use it, for example, when explaining a game or the meaning of a song.

Language summary

	Functional areas	Expressions*	Vocabulary*
Steps 1–15	Identification Quantity	*Look/Look at* *I am, it is* *What is this?* *Is it a . . . ? Yes/No* *How many?*	Small letters *a–s* Numbers *1–6* Nouns beginning with *a–s*
Steps 16–30	Description	*What colour is . . . ?* *What is this word/ letter/number?* *Point to . . .*	Small letters *t–z* Nouns beginning with *t–z* Classroom objects Colours *big/little*
Steps 31–45	Possession	*I have, Sue has* *How old are you?*	Toys *my*
Steps 46–60	Revision of Steps 1–45	Revision of Steps 1–45	Numbers *7–10* Parts of the body Shapes

*At the back of this book there is a complete list of the words used in the text of the Pupil's Book.
The Teacher's Book gives full guidance on the language syllabus and its presentation to the pupils.

Oxford University Press
Great Clarendon Street, Oxford OX2 6DP

Oxford New York

Athens Auckland Bangkok Bogota Bombay
Buenos Aires Calcutta Cape Town Dar es Salaam
Delhi Florence Hong Kong Istanbul Karachi
Kuala Lumpur Madras Madrid Melbourne
Mexico City Nairobi Paris Singapore
Taipei Tokyo Toronto

and associated companies in
Berlin Ibadan

OXFORD and OXFORD ENGLISH
are trade marks of Oxford University Press

ISBN 0 19 433912 2

© Oxford University Press 1988

First published 1988
Nineteenth impression 1996

Illustrated by Ray and Corinne Burrows

Printed in Hong Kong

STEP I
Look and say

Sue   Jack

⊡ Song

Hello song

Hello, hello, hello.
Hello, hello, hello.
Hello, hello, hello.
I am Sue.

Hello, hello, hello.
Hello, hello, hello.
Hello, hello, hello.
I am Jack.

STEP 2
Letters

a

apple

b

bird

 Song

Goodbye song

Goodbye Jack and Sue.
Goodbye Jack.
Goodbye Sue.
Goodbye Jack and Sue.
Goodbye Jack and Sue.

STEP 3

Letters

c

cat

d

dog

Numbers

1 • 2 : 3 ⋮

STEP 4

😑 Rhyme

One bird

Two birds

Three birds

CAT!

One cat

Two cats

Three cats

DOG!

1

2

3

1

2

3

STEP 5

Letters

e

elephant

f

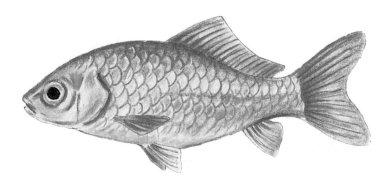

fish

g

girl

STEP 6

Rhyme

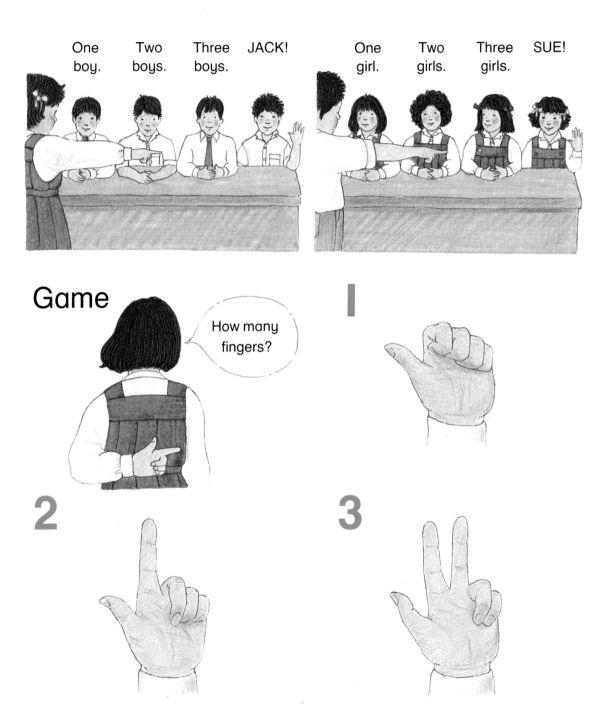

One boy. Two boys. Three boys. JACK!

One girl. Two girls. Three girls. SUE!

Game

How many fingers?

I

2

3

Letters

h

hand

i

insect

j

jug

STEP 8

Elephants and fishes

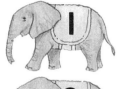

How many elephants?
Elephants, elephants.
How many elephants?
One, two, three.

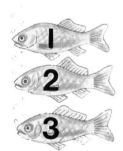

How many fishes?
Fishes, fishes.
How many fishes?
One, two, three.

Hello elephants!
Hello fishes!
Elephants and fishes.
One, two, three.

STEP 9
Numbers

1 2 3 4 5 6

📻 Song

Listen to the numbers

One, two, three,
Clap, clap, clap.
(×3)
Listen to the numbers.

1 2 3

Four, five, six.
Tap, tap, tap.
(×3)
Listen to the numbers.

4 5 6

One, two, three,

Four, five, six.

Clap, clap, clap.

Tap, tap, tap.

One, two, three,

Four, five six.

Listen to the numbers.

1 2 3
4 5 6

1 2 3 4 5 6

STEP 10

Picture practice

Show me a bird.
How many cats?

STEP 11
Letters

k

kite

l

lion

m

monkey

STEP 12

🎵 Song

How many monkeys?

How many monkeys?
One! One!
How many monkeys?
One monkey!

How many lions?
Two! Two!
How many lions?
Two lions!

How many insects?
Three! Three!
How many insects?
Three insects!

How many fishes?
Four! Four!
How many fishes?
Four fishes!

How many fingers?
Five! Five!
How many fingers?
Five fingers!

How many apples?
Six! Six!
How many apples?
Six apples!

1

2

3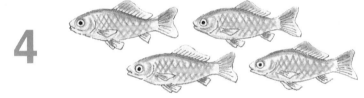

4

5

6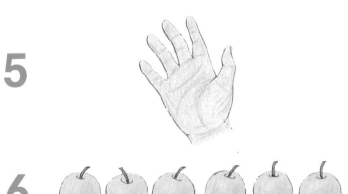

STEP 13

Letters

n

nest

o

orange

p

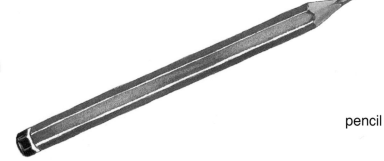

pencil

STEP 14

Game

Look at number 4.
Is it a monkey? *No!*
Is it a girl? *No!*
Is it a boy? *Yes!*

1  finger/insect/pencil

2 cat/dog/lion

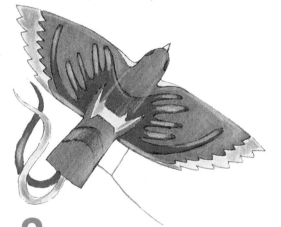

3 bird/insect/kite

4 monkey/girl/boy

5 fish/insect/elephant

6 orange/jug/apple

STEP 15

Letters

queen

robot

sun

STEP 16

🎞 Game

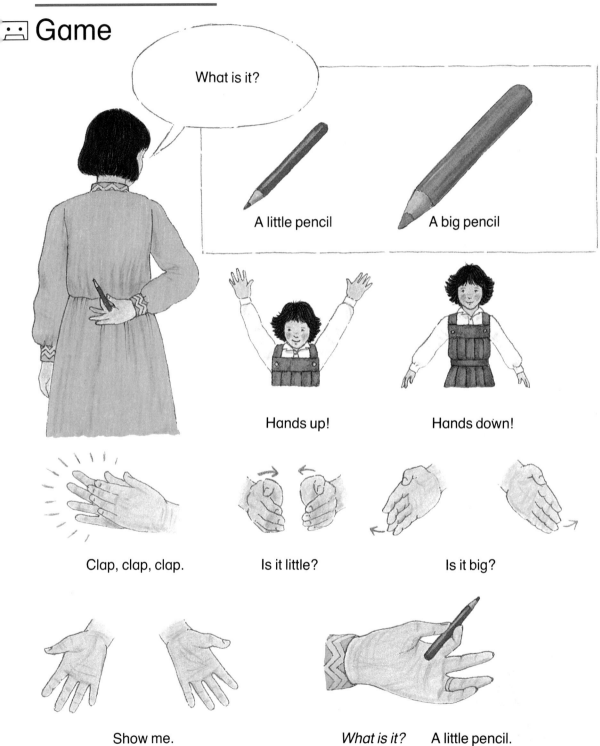

What is it?

A little pencil

A big pencil

Hands up!

Hands down!

Clap, clap, clap.

Is it little?

Is it big?

Show me.

What is it?   A little pencil.

STEP 17

Look and say

Point to a . . .

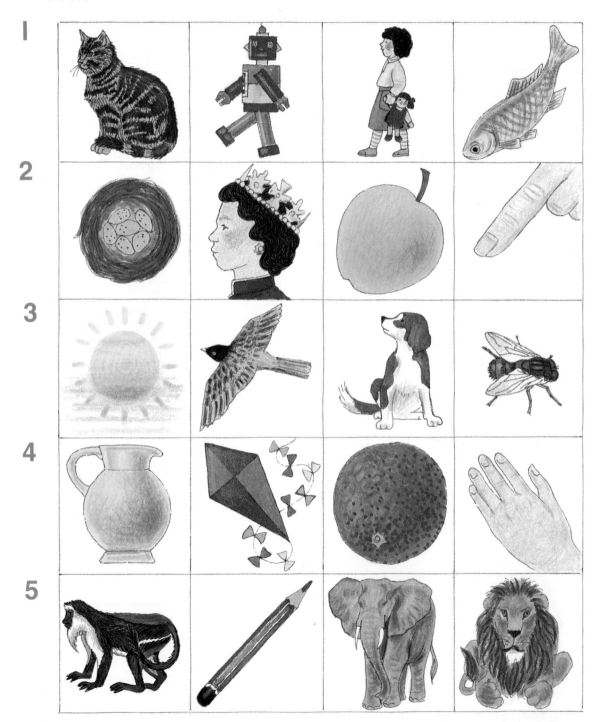

STEP 18

Picture practice

Look at robot number two.
Is it a big robot?

🎵 Song

Little girl, little boy

Sue is a little girl.
Look at Sue.
Jack is a little boy.
Look at Jack.
Little girl, little girl,
Look at Sue.
Little boy, little boy,
Look at Jack.

STEP 19

Letters

t

tree

u

umbrella

v

van

STEP 20

Look and say

a red umbrella

a green umbrella

a blue umbrella

🎴 Song

Sue's umbrella

Show me blue and show me red.
Look at a blue sky,
And look at Sue's umbrella.

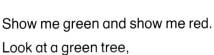

Show me green and show me red.
Look at a green tree,
And look at Sue's umbrella.

Sun up, sun down, show me red.
Look at a red sky,
And look at Sue's umbrella.

STEP 21

Letters

W

x

y

z

window

x-ray

yellow

ZOO ▶

zoo

STEP 22

Picture practice

Show me a big monkey.
Is it blue?
Show me a green van.

Read

red

blue

green

yellow

STEP 24

Alphabet song

a b c d e f g

h i j k l m n

o p q r s t u

v w

x y z

STEP 25

 Song   **Listen to the letters**

a for apple

b for bird

c for cat

d for dog

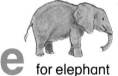
e for elephant

f for fish

Listen to the letters.

g for girl

h for hand

i for insect

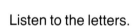
j for jug

k for kite

l for lion

Listen to the letters.

m for monkey

n for nest

o for orange

p for pencil

q for queen

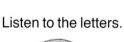
r for robot

Listen to the letters.

s for sun

t for tree

u for umbrella

v for van

w for window

x for x-ray

y for yellow

z for zoo

STEP 26

Sing a little song,
Sing a little song,

One, two, three.

Point to a window.

Point to a door.

Point to the ceiling.

Point to the floor.

FLOOR!
CEILING!
DOOR!
CEILING!

STEP 27

Look and say

an orange van

a brown van

a black van

a white van

Look and say

1

2

STEP 28

🎞 Rhyme

 One, two,

Red and blue.

 Up and down,

Yellow and brown.

 Bow to a queen,

Orange and green.

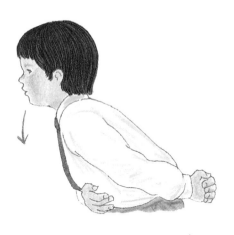

 Look at a kite,

Black and white.

black

orange

brown

white

STEP 30

Look and say

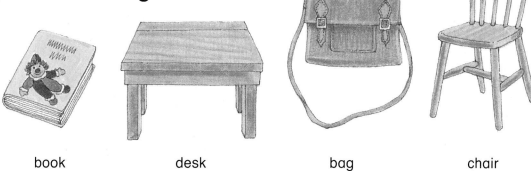

book   desk   bag   chair

Picture practice

STEP 31
Look and say

Sue has . . .
a bike
a ball
a doll

Jack has . . .
a kite
a book
a cat

STEP 32

⊡ Song

A red doll

I am Sue, I have a bike

And I have a red doll.

I am Sue, I have a ball,

A ball, a bike, a red doll.

I am Jack, I have a kite

And I have a black cat.

I am Jack, I have a book,

A book, a kite, a black cat.

STEP 33

Jack and Meg

1 Jack has a black cat.
   Listen . . .

2 *Miaow.*
   Hello. I am Meg.

3 Look. Jack has a big bed.

4 Meg has a little bed.

STEP 34

⊡ Song

I am a little boy

I am a little boy,

Hello, hello.

I have a little cat,

I have a cat,

I have a little cat.

I am a little cat,

Miaow, miaow.

I have a little bed,

I have a bed,

I have a little bed.

STEP 35

Read

book

kite

doll

ball

STEP 36

The big bag song

I have two kites,
I have two kites,
And a big bag.

I have three dolls,
I have three dolls,
Two kites,
And a big bag.

I have four balls,
I have four balls,
Two kites,
Three dolls,
And a big bag.

I have five books,
I have five books,
Two kites,
Three dolls,
Four balls,
And a big bag.

STEP 37

Yo-Yo's house

1 Sue has a red doll.
Listen . . .

2 Hello. I am Yo-Yo.

3 Yo-Yo has a little house.
Look.
Yo-Yo has a table.
Yo-Yo has a chair.

STEP 38

Yo-Yo's song

I have a chair,
And I have a bed.
It is my house,
It is my house.

It is my chair,
And it is my bed.
It is my house.

I have a table,
And I have a jug.
It is my house,
It is my house.

It is my table,
And it is my jug.
It is my house.

STEP 39

Look and say

train

plane

car

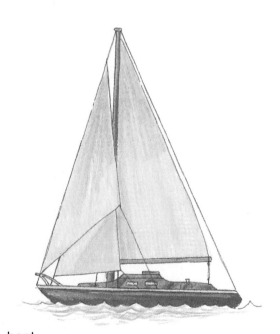

boat

STEP 40

📼 Song

Zoom zoom my plane

I have a car,
Brum, brum, my car.
Listen to my little car.

I have a car,
Brum, brum, my car,
My car, brum, brum, my car.

I have a train,
Chug, chug, my train.
Listen to my little train.

I have a train,
Chug, chug, my train,
My train, chug, chug, my train.

I have a plane,
Zoom, zoom, my plane.
Listen to my little plane.

I have a plane,
Zoom, zoom, my plane,
My plane, zoom, zoom, my plane.

STEP 41

Sue . . .
How old are you?
I am six.

Yo-Yo . . .
How old are you?
I am three.

Jack . . .
How old are you?
I am five.

Meg . . .
How old are you?
I am two.

STEP 42

🎴 Songs

It is my birthday

I am six. Yes, I am, I am.
I am six. Yes, I am, I am.
I am six. Yes, I am, I am.
I am a big girl.
It is my birthday.

I am five. Yes, I am, I am.
I am five. Yes, I am, I am.
I am five. Yes, I am, I am.
I am a big boy.
It is my birthday.

Happy birthday to you

Happy birthday to you,
Happy birthday to you,
Happy birthday, dear . . . ,
Happy birthday to you.

Step 43
Look and say

cake

balloon

hat

present

STEP 44

A present

X2 is a little robot.
X2 has a birthday.

Hello, X2. Happy birthday.
Here is a present.

Thank you.
What is it?

It is a doll . . . a robot-doll!

STEP 45
Picture practice

STEP 46

Read

car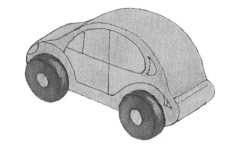

boat

plane

train

STEP 47

Numbers

1 2 3 4 5 6

7

8

9

10

STEP 48

Ten little robots

One little,
Two little,
Three little robots.

1 2 3

Four little,
Five little,
Six little robots.

4 5 6

Seven little,
Eight little,
Nine little robots.

7 8 9

Ten little robot-boys.

10

(Repeat with robot-girls)

STEP 49

Game

Is it a car?
Is it a red car?
Is it number seven?

STEP 50

Rhyme

1 2

One, two,
Look at my shoe.

3 4

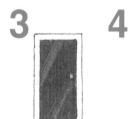

Three, four,
Point to a door.

5 6

Five, six,
Pick up sticks.

7 8

Seven, eight,
Open a gate.

9 10

Nine, ten,
A yellow hen.

STEP 51

Look and say

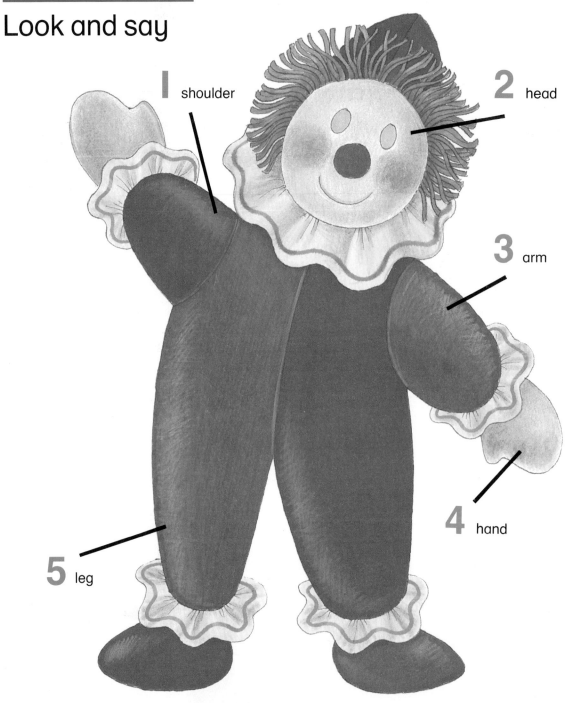

1 shoulder

2 head

3 arm

4 hand

5 leg

STEP 52

Song

It is my head

It is my head, my shoulders and my legs,

And my legs.

My head, my shoulders and my legs.

My head, my shoulders and my legs.

My head, my shoulders and my legs.

It is my hands, my fingers and my arms,

And my arms.

My hands, my fingers and my arms.

My hands, my fingers and my arms.

My hands, my fingers and my arms.

STEP 53

Game

My robot has red legs.

Is it X9?

No.

Is it X7?

Yes.

STEP 54

 Song

I am a robot

I am a robot,
Look at my arms,
Look at my arms,
Look at my arms.
I am a robot,
Look at my arms.
My arms go up and down.

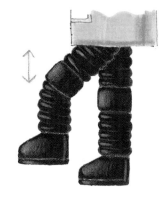

I am a robot,
Look at my legs,
Look at my legs,
Look at my legs.
I am a robot,
Look at my legs.
My legs go up and down.

I am a robot,
Look at my head,
Look at my head,
Look at my head.
I am a robot,
Look at my head.
My head goes up and down.

STEP 55

Four boxes

1

Jack has a lion,
a monkey and an elephant.

2

Sue has a bear.

3

Sue has four boxes.

4

Look. It is a zoo.

a bear

a monkey

a lion

an elephant

STEP 57

Look and say

square

circle

triangle

⊡ Song

Two sweets

I have two sweets in my **bag**,
A white triangle and a yellow square.
I have two sweets in my **hand**,
A white triangle and a yellow square.
I have two sweets in my **mouth** . . .
Mmm . . .

I have two sweets in my **bag**,
A yellow circle and an orange square.
I have two sweets in my **hand**,
A yellow circle and an orange square.
I have two sweets in my **mouth** . . .
Mmm . . .

STEP 58
Game

Look at number two.
How many triangles?
How many blue triangles?

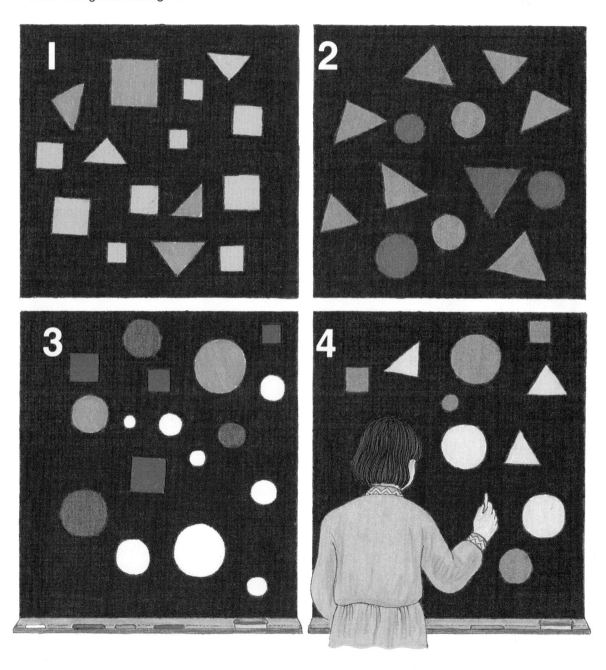

STEP 59
Picture practice

STEP 60

Game

Is it a letter?
Is it a blue letter?
Is it 'm'?

a	m	q	7
s	q	x	k
m	k	a	7
8	x	10	8
s	7	k	10

Word list

(Numbers indicate the step in which the word is first used in the text of the Pupil's Book)

10	a	9	four	13	pencil
24	alphabet	50	gate	50	pick up
1	am	5	girl	39	plane
17	an	54	go, goes	17	point to
2	and	2	goodbye	43	present (*noun*)
2	apple	20	green	15	queen
51	arm	7	hand	20	red
30	bag	42	happy birthday	15	robot
31	ball	31	has	47	seven
43	balloon	43	hat	50	shoe
55	bear	32	have	51	shoulder
33	bed	51	head	10	show me
16	big	1	hello	26	sing
31	bike	50	hen	9	six
2	bird	44	here	20	sky
44	birthday	37	house	2	song
27	black	6	how many?	57	square
20	blue	41	how old?	50	stick (*noun*)
39	boat	1	I	15	sun
30	book	57	in	57	sweet (*noun*)
28	bow (*verb*)	7	insect	37	table
55	box	18	is	9	tap (*verb*)
6	boy	14	is it?	47	ten
27	brown	38	it	44	thank you
43	cake	7	jug	9	the
39	car	11	kite	3	three
3	cat	51	leg	9	to
26	ceiling	25	letter (alphabet)	39	train
30	chair	11	lion	19	tree
57	circle	9	listen	57	triangle
9	clap	16	little	3	two
30	desk	14	look at	19	umbrella
3	dog	11	monkey	16	up
31	doll	57	mouth	19	van
26	door	38	my	44	what?
16	down	13	nest	27	white
47	eight	47	nine	21	window
5	elephant	14	no	21	x-ray
6	finger	9	number	21	yellow
5	fish	3	one	14	yes
9	five	27	orange (*adjective*)	21	zoo
26	floor	13	orange (*noun*)		
25	for	50	open		